Own Your Day, Own Your Life

Creating the business and life you desire

Brianne Showman, PT, DPT

ISBN: 978-1-7338177-1-4
ISBN: 978-1-7338177-2-1

Acknowledgements

This book was possible because of the many amazing people in my life. The people who gave me the inspiration and passion to write it. The people who have helped me to become the person I am today. The necessary people to make this book what it is today.

All the clinicians and colleagues with whom I spoken over the years in order to help you improve your focus, your feelings of overwhelm, and to improve how you get things done. This was created because of those many conversations.

To my SSPT Elite Family, listening to your stories gave me the passion to create this, both for you and for the many other business owners I know who are dealing with the same thing.

My coaches, Greg Todd and Ernie Welsh, you have helped me to become the person I am today. I couldn't have done this without you!

My editor, Trey Kauffman, and designer, Michelle Merz, thank you for all of your hard work!

I appreciate you all more than you know. Thank you!

Table of Contents

Section 1: Creating Me 1

   Chapter 1: Overworked 2

   Chapter 2: Finding Strategies 5

   Chapter 3: Learning Acceptance 7

   Chapter 4: Boss Vs Employee 9

Section 2: Creating Your Day 15

   Chapter 5: Know Your Focus 16

   Chapter 6: Organize Your Day…And Your Life 19

   Chapter 7: Creating Your Schedule 26

   Chapter 8: Tips And Tricks 27

Section 3: Creating Your Life.......................................31

   Chapter 9: Give Yourself Rules 32

   Chapter 10: Do Only The Things That Serve You ...35

   Chapter 11: Personal Development 41

   Chapter 12: Self-Care 45

Section 4: Creating Your Mindset...............................63

   Chapter 13: Create YOUR World 65

   Chapter 14: Create A Grateful Mind 73

Section 5: Now Go Create!...75

Afterward 77

References 79

Section 1: Creating Me

Why should you listen to me? Great question! I am a human with my strengths and weaknesses, failures and successes, just like anyone else. I am very Type A, like most business owners are. And just like most business owners, I began my business by working nearly 24/7. Okay, technically 20/7, as I did sleep for four hours a night.

I figured out how to overcome these issues, become more productive by working fewer hours.

This is my story. This is how I did it, and this is how I am still doing it every day.

Chapter 1: Overworked

As I was starting my business, I was working full-time as a physical therapist for a successful local outpatient physical therapy clinic. I was also the clinic director, overseeing the entire staff at the location, as well as the compliance specialist for the entire company. I was putting in 60+ hours a week as a full-time employee.

I spent my days either in patient care or doing administrative tasks at my full time job while my evenings and nights were occupied with other business building tasks. I had books to read on the regulations regarding Medicare and cash pay physical therapy, online classes for the ins and outs of a cash pay practice, and online classes for direct marketing for physical therapy practices. I was learning how to run a business since I had no business background and therefore no clue how to do such a thing. In whatever time I had left, I was seeing clients for my business as a side gig.

Because fitness is such a major part of my life and a part of my client niche, there was no way I was letting that part of my life slide. Besides, exercise and my training was the way I stayed sane, it was my stress relief. I was fine, though. I didn't feel exhausted. I was functioning at a high level. I was mentally sound. Or so I thought.

I never reached a breaking point like some people do, but I know I was the lucky one. Or perhaps I did and it went unnoticed, forcing me into bed early on Friday nights.

In January of 2017, I opened my brick and mortar practice. It was at that time I left the security of my full-time job and became a part-time contract worker. I knew it was still going to take time to build my business and would require a steady income, even if it was less. Aside from that, they were having difficulty finding a replacement since I was the clinic director. I remained the clinic director for another six months. I also stayed on as the compliance specialist.

I still felt good. No issues I was aware of.

In July of 2017, my clinic director duties were replaced. Even then, I was still committing to 15-20 hours a week of contract work and chart audits while working on my business as much as my body would allow.

Eighteen months after I had transitioned to a part-time contract position, I was still working 80 hours per week. I was still the only one working on my business. And to add to this, I was going through a divorce, sleeping on a friend's couch. My life was in flux, but I was even more determined to make it successful. Especially considering I was down to just my business for income. So I continued grinding away, sleeping just four hours per night.

It is crazy what adrenaline will let you do, and for how long!

Fast-forward to today, 21 months into becoming an entrepreneur, I am starting to figure it out. I now understand what my business coach had been talking about all this time. I realize my business will not fail because I decide to shut off for the night. I truly understand I don't need to be the one doing everything. I figured out how to find the interns or employees who are able to do the simple, delegable tasks. I finally realized there are ways I can work 40 hours a week instead of 80.

I've started sleeping more, now getting six hours of shut-eye a night. It may not be ideal for most, but it is ideal for me. Now that I am sleeping more, I look back and wonder how I survived for over a year on four hours of sleep. It also makes me realize my health was not what I thought it was. Being that I was running on adrenaline non-stop, my cortisol levels were certainly off. Since improving my sleep, my mindset, and determining to work less, my training and performance has improved significantly.

I also realized I had not been dealing with life's stressors as well as I thought I had been. Mental breakdowns were a frequent occurrence when simple things didn't go as planned—and I am talking simple. A bad workout. Something not going right with a computer software. Simple things broke me. I was a mental mess due to the increased stress, my lack of sleep, and my hormones being out of control.

I am a medical professional whose job it is to help humans improve their quality of life, but I wasn't paying attention to my own. What a lesson that was.

Chapter 2: Finding Strategies

Living a life of being overworked, over-stressed, overwhelmed, and over-committed is not an ideal situation. Everyone can live there for awhile, but eventually it catches up to all of us. We either experience burnout, mental breakdowns, or health issues. Maybe all of the above. You never know what your body and mind may decide to do at any given time when you aren't giving it what it needs.

I was living the overworked and over-committed life. In order to pay the bills and build my business, it was something I had to do. Or so I thought. It never occurred to me there was perhaps a different way, a way that would be less stressful and less time consuming.

The hours I was working weren't going to be changing for the foreseeable future, so something else had to change in order for me to decrease my stress levels and decrease the overwhelm I was experiencing.

By this time, I had two incredible coaches, one business coach and one life coach. When I hired them, I failed to anticipate what I would go through in the coming months. They are the most important investments I have ever made.

I've worked with my life coach to create strategies to avoid feeling overwhelmed. Simple things which have been very effective in my life. Strategies I use frequently when my to-do list adds up. When I start feeling the mental frustration due to having so many things to do in a single day, I learned to create my list, prioritize it, and take action.

When I first began my coaching journey, I didn't expect it to have as much of an impact as it did. I was amazed at how effective it was, not just from the standpoint of feeling less overwhelmed, but also with how successful I have become in completing tasks.

When I use this strategy, I tend to get through my tasks in half the time. All of a sudden everything is done and I am left asking myself, "Now what?" Everything is done for the day and I have time for myself, time I was not expecting to have.

My business coach has helped me to learn when and how to say "no". Early on in my business, I would say "yes" to nearly every possible opportunity. I was grasping at straws in order to make things happen. I needed money. I needed clients. I needed a plan to bring them in the door. That was before I had my coaches. When I hired my business coach, he helped me to find the right path. Eventually, I understood that I needed to say no to things which didn't support the vision I had for my business, to things that did not serve my business and did not serve me. If it was something that was not directly related to my niche demographic, then it was not worth my time or energy.

Both coaches helped with the mindset aspect of that. They helped me understand that I don't "need" anything. They taught me I can create anything I want, it's just a matter of how I do it. It comes down to how I serve people and meet their needs. Focusing on my needs was not successful; focusing on other people's needs is what changed everything, for me mentally and financially.

I have learned countless other strategies for dealing with life which I implement on a daily basis, but those mentioned were the ones that were the biggest game changers to break me out of not only feeling overworked, but actually being overworked.

Chapter 3: Learning Acceptance

It took me 21 months, but I finally learned to accept things would be OK if I was not working constantly. It was a long process, though. It was something I had been working on for the eight months prior. It was something I *knew* I had to work on while I was doing it, but it wasn't until I fully accepted it that I made the progress, that I had the mindset shift.

I'll tell you what, habits are hard to change, but mindset is a whole other ball game. It is one of the most difficult things I have ever had to work on, and continue to work on every single day!

First and foremost, I learned my business would not fail if I allowed myself to shut down for the night and stop working at a normal time. I learned that if I didn't respond to messages in the evening, they would still be there in the morning. Even more important was that people wouldn't be mad if I didn't respond late at night and that I wouldn't lose clients by not responding to messages after normal working hours.

Guess what? Those things I thought had to be done that night. They didn't. They were still there the next day, just waiting for me. They didn't have deadlines, only the deadlines I was putting on them because I felt they needed them.

Once I learned how to shut down in the evenings, how to work less, I began to learn it was perfectly fine to take my time if I needed it. As I stated earlier, I was going through a divorce and things in my life were crazy. Most times, I used my work to take my mind off the negative. Occasionally things would get rough and I needed the mental break. It was a somewhat forced break by my colleague and my business coach at first, both of whom were telling me to take some time for myself. I did it because I knew I wasn't in a place to focus on my work, but I did it reluctantly as I knew I was avoiding things which needed to be done. As time went on, I realized how important this "me time" was and still continues to be. I now take breaks daily for myself, only it's now different. I take 5-10 minutes to meditate and to breathe, just to relax my brain, which gives me a good mental reset and recharge. It's not only good for me mentally, but physically as well.

It was a long process to learn and accept shutting down and taking breaks for myself, but it was one of the most important things I have learned for both myself and for my business.

Chapter 4: Boss Vs Employee

As a business owner, especially starting out, I did everything. I played the role of President, Human Resources, Bookkeeper, Marketer, Content Creator, Social Media Specialist, Video Editor, and Physical Therapist. I'm sure I'm leaving some roles out. I was doing everything.

So why was I doing everything? Several reasons. First and foremost, I didn't know any better. I didn't have the money to pay someone to work for me, I thought this was how small business started, and I knew I could do most tasks better than someone else could. Did I say I didn't know any better? That was the biggest factor. I hadn't found my network or coach yet to teach me differently.

Eventually, I started to figure things out. I started to learn there are better ways to do things. I still wasn't quite comfortable giving up tasks, partially because I didn't know where to find people, but I was at least able to create systems for myself, albeit slowly. I am still perfecting those systems and creating new ones daily. It is a constant process which will never end as I continue to grow the company.

I eventually started outsourcing, letting go of the one task I knew I didn't do well — video editing. I wanted to make my videos look more professional, and I knew someone who could do it. I can't say I would have gotten rid of that task had I not known someone whom I trusted. The time had come for me to start paying someone for work. EEK! I didn't think I had the money to do it, but when I considered how long it would take me to do the editing as I wanted it to be done, and how much my time is worth, it made perfect sense. That was the beginning of my shift in mindset.

It wasn't until a year later I actually started paying someone else to join my team. This time, I knew I had to. I was taking on a project way beyond my area of expertise. I knew the subject matter and could create the content, but needed someone to edit the videos. More than anything, I didn't know the ins and outs of the platform I would be using. I could take many hours learning it by trial and error until I was able to create the product I wanted, or I could hire someone who could do it in half the time and whom I could pay a significant amount less than my hourly rate. It just made sense. It was then when I hired my amazing Virtual Assistant team. They are incredible at what they do and have been a huge time saver for me. I was starting to value myself, my time, my worth. It took a long time for me to understand and appreciate my worth as a business owner and to outsource those big tasks which were chipping away at my day.

I still wasn't fully into the CEO mindset yet, but I was getting closer. My coach and colleagues had been talking to me for months about finding an intern for simple tasks. They would tell me there are a lot of people who need marketing internships or just want to learn the social media side of things. I never did it. I felt it was going to be far too time consuming to both find someone to do it and to train them. About 21 months into my business, I realized there were simple tasks I could get rid of. There was no reason I needed to be handling my own social media, creating my own webpages, blog posts and Your Friday Fix videos, or even editing my podcast. These were simple tasks I could easily teach someone to do. I finally decided I needed an intern, and I was able to find one quickly. Using my coach's strategies, he was trained before I knew it. Within one week, I was asking myself why I had waited so long. If I would have just realized how much time it freed up for me to do the tasks only I could do for the business, I would have taken action much sooner. Lesson learned!

That lesson is why I also hired a part-time administrative assistant. I began thinking about other tasks, slightly more important than before, that I was spending time on which I could easily train someone to do. These were more on the Human Resources side of things, like inputting expenses and income, creating Profit & Loss statements, and doing market research. This was a much harder decision. It meant giving up more important tasks, giving up tasks I enjoy doing, it required more trust in the individual, and it gave me an employee, something else I needed to learn. Luckily, I had an accountant to teach me the legal side of having an employee.

Speaking of employees, I also learned from my coach that I needed to start acting like an employee at times, not just the boss. Employees have a schedule. Employees follow that schedule. Employees ask for time off when time off is needed. I wasn't doing that. I had a schedule, but I allowed myself to fluctuate from it. Someone unable to come in during my normal clinic hours? No problem, let's see where I can flex. Have a project I am working on? OK, let's work 20-hour days in order to get it done. You name it, I allowed myself to do it.

I already had my schedule created. I just had to make myself follow it. I had to remember to value myself, value my time, value my worth. Once I started reminding myself of that, I had less difficulty being the employee. I also started to set rules for myself in the evening. Employees don't work until crazy hours of the night (most times). It was time for me to stop doing that as well. As I mentioned in the previous chapter, the work would still be there in the morning. Messages could be responded to then. Even though in my head I thought not responding would lose me a client, I understood at the same time those individuals are like me — they send messages when they think about something, not necessarily expecting a response during non-work hours.

It has been a long process, and it is still something I am working on, but I have at least started to learn how to be the CEO, the boss, the employee, and how to separate those roles.

The structure of my current delegation of tasks.

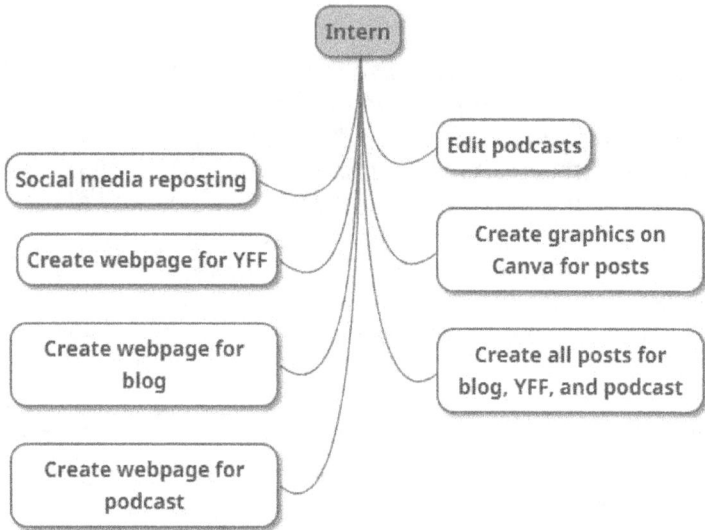

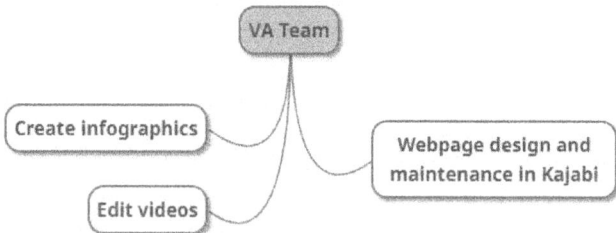

Intern

- Social media reposting
- Create webpage for YFF
- Create webpage for blog
- Create webpage for podcast
- Edit podcasts
- Create graphics on Canva for posts
- Create all posts for blog, YFF, and podcast

VA Team

- Create infographics
- Edit videos
- Webpage design and maintenance in Kajabi

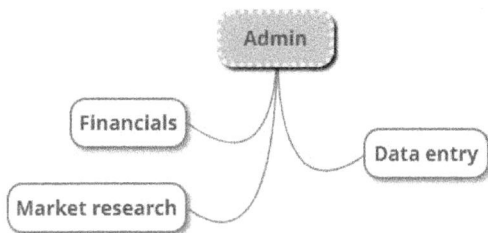

Admin
- Financials
- Market research
- Data entry

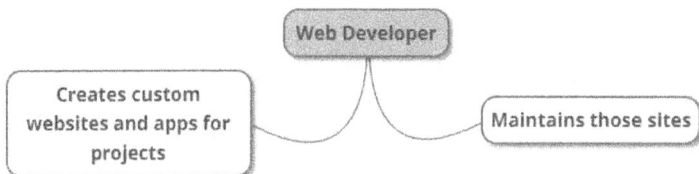

Web Developer
- Creates custom websites and apps for projects
- Maintains those sites

Section 2: Creating Your Day

Now you know my story. All the crazy ups and downs of my process beginning from full-time employee and the transition into business owner. It was a wild ride. OK, so it still is every single day. Some days are just more wild than others.

Let's get into how this whole process transpired. The strategies, tips, tricks, etc. that I used to become the person I am today.

Chapter 5: Know Your Focus

As a business owner, you have goals you want to meet. If you are like most business owners, you have yearly goals and quarterly goals. If you do as my coach has me do, you break those goals into monthly goals as well. The smaller the goal, the more attainable it seems.

Which sounds easier?
- $500K for the year
- $125K for the quarter
- $41.6K for the month

I will take that $41.6K for the month all day. When you break it down that way, it makes the $500K goal seem much more feasible.

And within that income goal, you have your methods for getting there. Your methodology depends on what industry you are in, but every business has their product or service. Based on those products and services, you plan new things for the year — new packages, new products, new services, new strategies, etc.

From this yearly and monthly plan, you can figure out what your focus is on a weekly basis. The more you break goals down into digestible pieces, the easier the whole process is. Ask yourself, what is the one task that when you complete it, it will help you achieve several wins, help you move onto the next step, will progress you toward your goals? You can have several different focuses based on time frame. I have found great success by doing a weekly focus which I break down into daily focuses.

So what does this look like for you?

Look at your yearly, quarterly, and monthly goals. Based on those goals, figure out what your next step will be. What is the most impactful thing you can do next? If you are working on a project, what is that next step you need to complete to move forward? If your goal is client acquisition, what needs to be done to find those new leads? Taking time to figure out what will make the biggest difference for that coming week is helpful when creating your schedule, which we will get to in upcoming chapters.

Yearly Goals •••	Q1 Goals •••
$500K gross income	$125K gross income
$250K of gross income is passive/residual	$62.5K gross income is passive/residual
200 new clients	50 new clients
Online course/platform created and launched.	Create videos for course/platform
+ Add another card	+ Add another card

January Goals •••	Habits to reach goals •••
$42K gross income	Make a plan
$21K of gross income is passive/residual	Reach out to 10 people a day
	Create a schedule daily
17 new clients	Do 1 hour of focused content creation work daily.
Create mind map for course/platform	
+ Add another card	Turn off notifications
	Get 7 hours of sleep each night
	+ Add another card

Example on how to set up your goals.

Once you figure out your weekly focus, you can figure out what your daily focus will be. As Ryan Munsey says in *F*ck Your Feelings*[1], find the one task each day that will "move the chains." By consistently completing tasks each day to move you closer toward your goal, you will find success. Does this guarantee you will meet your goals? Of course not. Nothing is ever guaranteed when it comes to goals. But what it does do is it guarantees you are moving forward in the process rather than staying stagnant or moving backward.

Chapter 6: Organize Your Day...And Your Life

I can't say where I learned to be organized, just that I was born with it. It's difficult for me to remember a time in my life when I wasn't. I know it sounds crazy, but it's true. Both in a "where things are kept" sense and from a scheduling sense, I have always been organized. I will admit, I am a little (read: a lot) O.C.D. when it comes to this.

From a "things" standpoint, everything needs to have its place. It drives me nuts to not be able to find something quick and easy. Even when I was little, each of my toys and books had their proper place. To this day, everything has its place and everything is put back when I am done using it. As I got older, this continued into books, schoolwork, documents, paperwork, etc. When talking about paperwork and documents, those all need to be filed in a system that makes sense as well. Or at least it has to make sense to me. In high school, I called it my "organized mess" for a while. I didn't have a desk or a filing system, so everything was on my floor, in piles, in an orderly fashion. Eventually my mom bought me a crate with hanging folders to keep my files and things for school in so I could get it all off the floor. I have a different methodology now, but I continue to use systems that work for me to keep track of where everything is.

Every person is going to have a different system when it comes to filing, both on the computer and in paper form. The important thing is to find something that works for you. My system may not make sense to other people, just like other people's systems don't make sense to me. I had a boss in the past who had the most unorganized desk I had ever seen, but ask her where something was and she could find it in a matter of seconds.

If you don't have employees and you are the only one who needs to find the documents, then find a system that works for you and use it. As you grow, that system will need to be modified or enhanced, which is totally normal. I've had to change mine over the past couple years as well.

If you have employees who need to access files and documents, work together to find a system that works for everyone. In order to operate efficiently and successfully, it is important to find a system that everyone can agree on. Notice I said agree and not love. Not everyone on a team will totally love a system that is in place, and that is fine. As long as everyone is willing to work within the system, adapt their ways for the benefit of the team, then your team will continue to run efficiently and effectively. That's not to say someone won't have a differing opinion. If they do, hear them out. It may be a good idea, it may be a bad idea. You won't know until you discuss it and think about it. Change is different, but different is not necessarily bad.

I was the one in school people would ask when deadlines were, when things were due, and when tests were. I kept track of everything! I still do. Only now, I have more to keep track of. Because of this, I have developed systems that have helped me to do this better and more efficiently. Systems that keep me from becoming overwhelmed by the crazy to-do list called my life. These are systems I have developed over time, both by trial and error as well as by learning concepts from people smarter than me.

I absolutely love my whiteboard. Every Sunday I write down the things I want to get done in both my business and in my personal life that week. I put everything down, from the smallest task that will take 10 minutes to the tasks which will take all week, if not longer. It is basically my giant to-do list for the week. (I love lists and I love to be able to check things off.)

On my whiteboard, I have notes and tasks separated into sections: Business, Partnerships, Projects, Personal, and my "one thing" for the week and day. As I said earlier, I am very O.C.D. when it comes to organizing things. This includes my schedule.

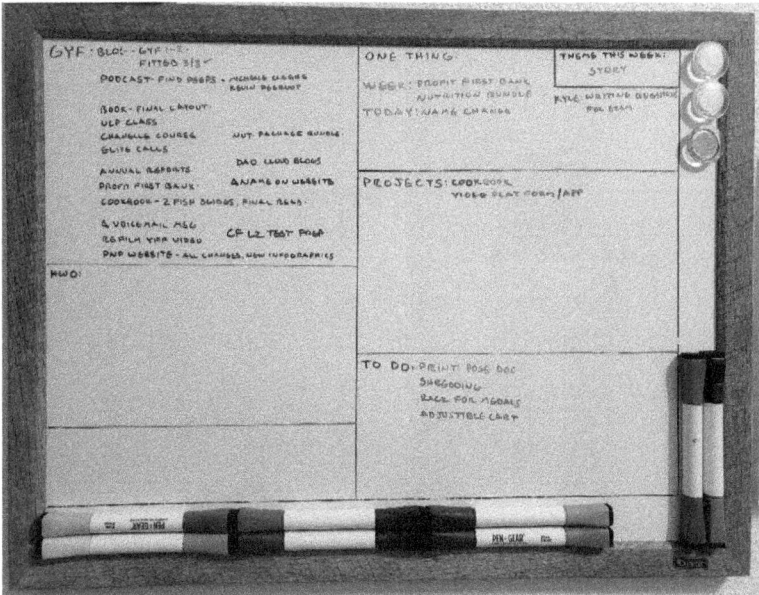

Creating my weekly plan.

You don't necessarily need a whiteboard for this; paper and pen work just fine. You can also utilize technology for this. There are a number of programs and apps you can use to organize and plan. Personally, I use Trello for organizing and planning my projects, especially projects I am working on with other people so we can share ideas and communicate easier. You can also use things like OneNote, Evernote, or any general "notebook" type of software to do this.

My One Thing for the week ...

Create bundle package and marketing messaging.

+ Add another card

My Intention for the week ...

Serve everyone in the way they want to be served.

+ Add another card

Must do this week ...

Create bundle package

Figure out messaging for each part of package

Write 3 blog posts

Call bank

Finish website updates (web developer)

Film video for website

+ Add another card

If I have time this week ...

Refilm series video

Find guests for podcast

Get caught up on FB Lives from coach

+ Add another card

Projects (current and upcoming) ...

Fitness app

Cookbook

+ Add another card

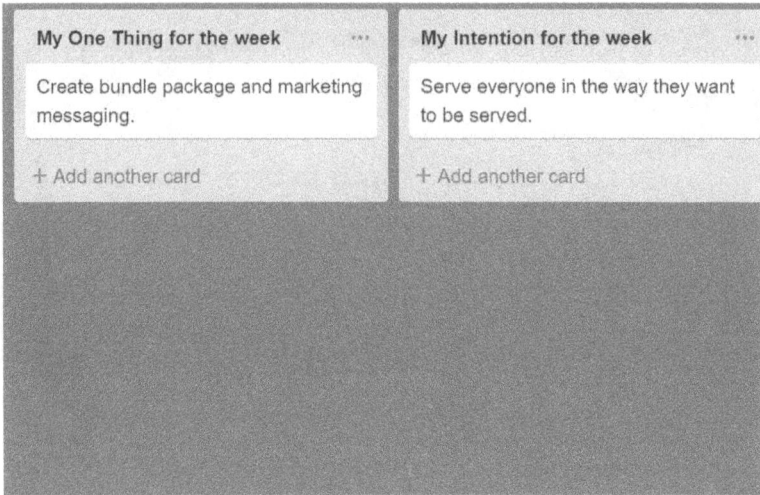

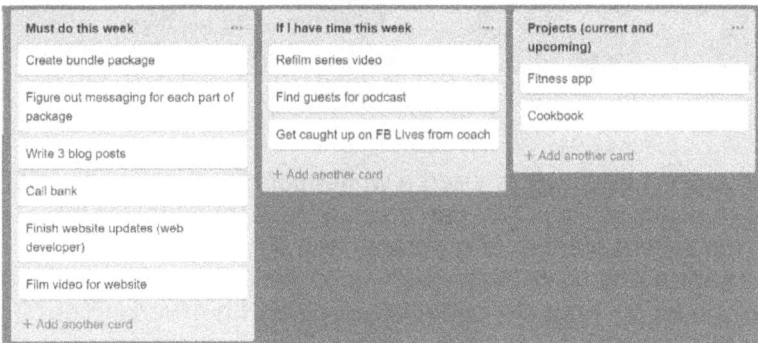

Trello board example.

When writing out your plans and goals for the week, remember these are all based on what your monthly and quarterly goals are. This is why setting those goals and focus, as discussed in Chapter 5, is so important. Once you have those created, it is much easier to plan out your weeks. Think about what projects you have deadlines for in the next couple of months, think about what your goals are. From there, break down your tasks and plan out your week.

Once you have all of your tasks written down, now it is time to prioritize them. Looking through your list, what needs to be accomplished sooner rather than later? Do any tasks have deadlines in the next day or two? Are any of them ongoing projects you are working on? It is necessary that you prioritize your tasks here in order to move forward. Sometimes it can help to put deadlines on tasks as well if they don't have them. If you actually give it a deadline, it can be easier to prioritize.

Once everything is prioritized, it will be easier to plan out your day. At this point, you don't need to plan out every day the entire week, only the following day. I do this by sitting down each evening to plan out my next day. Based on what I prioritized, I figure out what needs to be accomplished and and write down the next day's tasks.

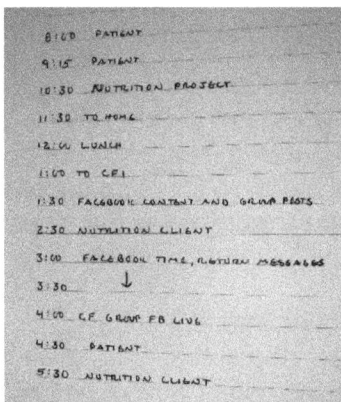

A typical Wednesday schedule   A typical Thursday schedule

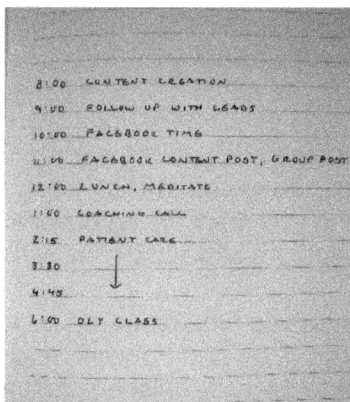

Now, here is the important part for staying focused and on task every single day: Time blocking. Time blocking is a game changer for keeping focused on your work. When you have a big list of things to get done, it can be difficult to keep your head on the task at hand without thinking about the other 10 things on the list. This is where time blocking is extremely helpful.

With time blocking, you literally plan out every hour of your day. In those blocks of time, you put down what you are going to be working on during that given time.

For example, mine may look something like this:
3:15-4:15 personal development
4:15-4:30 get ready for gym
4:30-4:45 drive time
4:45-6:15 gym time
6:15-7:30 drive time and get ready for day
7:30-8:30 chart reviews
8:30-9:30 write blog
9:30-10:30 follow up with leads and clients, emails
10:30-10:45 Facebook Live
10:45-12:00 film videos
12:00-12:30 lunch, meditation
12:30-4:30 patient care

Why is this important? If you know you are working on certain things during certain times, you don't think about the other things on the list. It is much easier to focus on the one thing you are working on when you already know the other things are already on the schedule for later in the day.

When you time block, do not go over time. If you gave yourself an hour to work on a task, stop at that hour, even if not technically finished. Just note you didn't finish it and add it to the list for tomorrow. The more you let yourself get off schedule, the more you will lose focus of the task at hand. Because of this, make sure you schedule the appropriate amount of time for your tasks. If you are working on payroll and you know it is going to take three hours, give yourself three hours in your time block.

The really cool thing with time blocking is many times you get done faster than you expected to. When you are focused on the task at hand and not thinking about everything else you have to do, you work more efficiently. When this happens, you have a couple options: 1) Keep a list going on the side of things you can tackle if you do have extra time, or

2) Take that 5-15 minutes to rest your brain. For me, I do both. I tend to stack my Monday and Tuesday when my brain is fresh, filling those extra spots with tasks. By Friday, I am wanting those breaks and take them.

When you are scheduling your day out in time blocking fashion, there are two things you want to think about. As much as possible, you'll want to put your task(s) that will "move the chains," as well as the task(s) that will take the most brain power and concentration, first. I do most of my content writing first, as that is when I am most creative, and then I do the task that will "move the chains." For me, that is what I have found is most effective. You may need to play with things a bit to figure out what is most effective for you.

Once you begin to time block and realize how much more focus you have in your day, you will never go back!

Chapter 7: Creating Your Schedule

In the previous chapter we discussed organizing, prioritizing, making a daily schedule, and time blocking. But what exactly do you put on the schedule? Everything! Literally, everything!

Most people think about their work schedules and their family schedules, those things the significant other and the kids have going on. What people forget to put on the schedule is those "other things" - those things that you intend to do, but never get to.

Here's the deal, if it is important to you, it needs to be on a schedule. (I choose my words wisely and don't use "need" lightly, so you know I mean business here!) The thing is, if it is not on the schedule, it won't happen. I know this first-hand. There are a lot of things in my past I neglected, my relationships being the biggest among them, because I did not schedule time for them to grow. I didn't understand how important it was to schedule everything important to me. I have since learned my lesson and am now working to rebuild the relationships I neglected for a long time.

Want a regular date night with your significant other? Schedule it! Want to create time to spend with your family? Schedule it! Want to get to the gym more? Schedule it! There is really no excuse for saying you don't have time for something. It is simply a matter of making it important, making it a priority, and putting it in your schedule.

Here's the most important part. Stick to your schedule! Yes, emergency situations happen, but those are also very rare. Unless it is an emergency, those things on the schedule are the most important things to focus on and pay attention to. You wouldn't put them on your schedule if they weren't important.

Chapter 8: Tips And Tricks

In this day and age, so many distractions exist to take attention away from the tasks at hand: notifications popping up on our phones and computers, getting lost scrolling through social media, and friends and family wanting our time. You name it, it is there to distract you. It may not even be something or someone, it may just be that you have difficulty focusing on the task at hand.

So how do you overcome the inability to stay focused? How do you control the distractions constantly being thrown at you? It is not an easy task, but there are some things you can do to minimize them and improve your focus.

It can be difficult when it comes to actual humans being the cause of the distraction, especially coworkers or family, but it is still possible if you approach it correctly.

Coworkers can be the toughest distraction to overcome, depending on your office situation. If you have a door you can shut, then it is a little easier. Shutting your door naturally keeps people from bothering you. If you still have coworkers or employees who are constantly knocking on your door, you can create rules that if the door is shut that means you are not to be disturbed. Most times, whatever people need can wait for an hour or two until you are available. If your office does not have a door, this can be a bit more tricky, but still possible. It can be helpful to create a set schedule for your "focus time." If you create focus time from 9:00-11:00, people will learn to value and respect your time, avoiding stopping in during those hours. They will quickly learn to talk to you before or after those times. If you do that, however, be fully attentive to them as they want to discuss business during those other times of the day.

If you work from home, it is important to set rules or create ways to notify your family that it is your working time. I have a colleague who works out of his home, which requires frequent conference calls and filming of videos. He has a fun

Disney sign he puts on the door so his two young girls know that he is working at the time and cannot come in and bother him. When the sign is down, he may still be working, but at the same time they know they are welcome to come in if they need something.

As far as significant others or spouses, it is important to communicate when working hours are if you work from home. This can be where the schedule comes in handy. If your significant other knows you have a date night or family time scheduled later, they will happily let you work during the hours you are scheduled to work, knowing they will get their time with you later.

If you are easily distracted by people in public, I would not advise attempting to work at coffee shops or restaurants. For me, I can easily focus on what I am working on, so I don't have a problem if I want to get out of my office and go somewhere for a bit. I have to actually remind myself to be more in the moment, aware of my surroundings, and approachable when in the community because I normally am so rushed and focused.

Now onto the technology side of things. First and foremost, turn the notifications off, both on your phone and your computer. The only notifications I have active on my phone are Facebook messenger, text message, and voicemail. I have all social media notifications turned off. There is no reason you need to know every time someone comments on a post or every time someone goes Live.

With those message notifications that are still active, the important thing is to not let them distract you. Schedule set times to respond to messages. If you respond to each message when it comes through, you will never get any work done. For example, set time at 8:00, 12:00, and 4:00 to respond to messages. If a message comes from a family member, glance at it to see if it's an emergency. If it isn't, it can wait as well.

Email should be the same as text and Facebook Messenger in regard to responding. Your email should not be always open. If it is, once again, you will likely not get any work done because you will be responding and putting out fires all day. Create set times when you will respond to email. For me, it is the same as my texting schedule. I will check my email at 8:00, 12:00, and 4:00. The only reason I may check my email more frequently is if I am expecting one to come through in order to complete what I am working on. If that's the case, I will check to see if that specific email has come through and ignore the rest until it is my scheduled time to take care of emails.

Schedule your social media time as well. It can be so easy to waste hours on social media scrolling through news feeds if you allow yourself to. Avoid that at all costs! This doesn't mean you can't be on it for enjoyment, but be cautious of how long you are spending on it when you do. For business purposes, schedule set times that you will be on social media. Personally, I get on between 4:00-4:30 AM and maybe again in the evening if I have time. When I am on, I check and respond to notifications on my business pages, in the groups I run, and then the other handful of groups I look at daily for business purposes. The only other time I am on during the day is to do my social media posting, but I get right off once I am done.

The easiest way to avoid all distractions when you want focused time is to either completely shut your phone off or to put it on airplane mode. When I am doing any writing or content creation, I put mine in airplane mode. I use this mode because there is an app I use that has music on it specifically for focusing (I will get into that more later), so I still need my phone to be on. Once I am done with those hours of focused work, I turn airplane mode off so any messages can come through. But, I still don't respond to those messages until the appropriate time.

I provided you a lot of tips and tricks for keeping focused during your day. Integrating these changes can be difficult, as can any change. I challenge you to start with one change within the next couple days and slowly add in more as the weeks go on. Before you know it, you will be more focused than ever.

Section 3: Creating Your Life

You can truly create the life that you want. You can create the time and the freedom to do the things you have been putting off doing, to do the new things you want to learn. You can spend time with your family without feeling like you are neglecting your business. Most importantly, you can improve your health — physical, mental, emotional.

This is the part that pulls you out of feeling burnt out, overworked, overstressed, overwhelmed, and brings you back to the happy person you remember being before you ever started your business.

Chapter 9: Give Yourself Rules

You may or may not have been a rule follower growing up. I know I was and I know the majority of business owners I have talked with were people who followed rules all throughout their lives.

Having rules gives structure. Having rules gives order. Rules bring you out of chaos and back to clarity. Rules can actually help calm your mind, especially when it is you who gets to make them!

As an employee, yes, there are things we don't like, but by the same token, life can be somewhat easier. As an employee, you know the rules, you know the standards, you follow those rules and standards. There is little thought into what you should do, as you already know what should be done in most circumstances.

When you are your own boss, that changes. I can speak from experience, as I did not have rules myself. I worked non-stop on my business: I answered emails and other messages whenever they came through, I lived on social media, never wanting to miss something which may cause me to lose a potential client, I worked on projects all hours of the night until I couldn't think coherently anymore, and I worked weekends in order to get more work done. I was running myself to the ground. Don't get me wrong, I loved what I was doing (and still do), which is why I was doing it. At no time did it ever feel like *work*. And on top of all of that, I still kept up with things around the house — maybe not to the standards I would have liked, but they were acceptable based on the fact I was working 80+ hours a week.

So why did I have to develop rules? Because I was destroying myself from the inside out, I just didn't realize it at the time. I was destroying relationships. And looking back, my performance at the gym was suffering as well.

When we have freedom in our business, we take advantage of that freedom, often times to our detriment. We do what we want, when we want. This means we work non-stop because we can; there is no one to tell us not to do it. Your spouse or significant other may say something, but this often is taken as nagging or forcing you to do what you don't want to do. It does not leave you in a good headspace if you stop because your loved one asks you to, it feels like an obligation rather than a choice.

As an employee, you are rewarded for overtime (sometimes). As your own boss, you feel you are rewarded indirectly. Your business will grow more if you work more, right? Wrong!

As your own boss, the only person who can tell you to stop is you! Which means it's time to set some rules.

You can create your own, but the ones I have set for myself are:
1. No social media after 7:00 pm.
2. No messaging (emails, texts, or Facebook Messenger) after 8:00 pm.
3. No screens after 8:30 pm. I don't watch TV, but this also includes e-readers or tablets. When I read in the evening, it is in paper form rather than digital. The only reason I go past 8:00 pm for screens is because my food log and my meditation app are on my phone.

In order to transition into these rules, it started with my five minute meditation when I got home each night in order to determine how tired my body and mind truly were. If I realized I was exhausted from the day during that five minutes of relaxing and breathing, then I was done working. If I found I had more energy, I would allow myself to continue working.

Your rules are going to be different, but for me, those are what I had to set. Before I did that, I would work until 9:00, then do my meal prep for the next day. By the time I would get to bed it would be 10:00 or later. I realized it was not healthy for me to live on that little amount of sleep. I shut down earlier than many of my colleagues do (and likely earlier than any of you do), but my goal is to be in bed by 8:30 and then journal and read until 9:00 at the absolute latest. When you wake up at 3:00 am, you have to shut down earlier!

Your rules may include time with your family every evening. Or maybe if you are working to get rid of a bad habit, you may create a rule that is related to that, such as only watching one hour of TV if you tend to watch two to three hours every night. You have to make the rules that will be best for you and your family. Your situation is unique to you, therefore your rules need to be unique to you.

Whatever your rules are, the important thing is to stick to them. You can set rules all you want, but if you constantly break them, it is not going to matter. Does this mean I stick to my rules 100% of the time? Not at all. Things happen. The nights I work as late as 7:30 with clients, if I have messages from clients that need to be responded to that day, then I'll respond. With that said, if it is not urgent and can wait until the next day, I push it to the next morning. It is not black and white, but I stick to it as much as I can.

Ultimately, the purpose of these rules is so you don't work 24/7. Or more importantly, so you don't feel like you have to work 24/7. Anyone can stop working if they choose to, but the guilt of not working or not responding to clients can be worse at times. I know business owners who had so much difficulty accepting not working constantly they turned to drinking in order to attempt to relax their brain and shut off work. Others I know have developed resentment of their significant others due to feeling forced to stop working, eventually leading to arguments. Over time, this all just leads to a downward spiral. Stop the spiral before it starts by setting rules for yourself.

Chapter 10: Do Only The Things That Serve You

Do only the things that serve you. Sounds a bit selfish, right? That's what I thought at first, too.

"If I do only the things that serve me, how will that help anyone else?"
"If I don't do things that serve my family, I will neglect them."
"If I don't serve my clients, I won't have a business."

Are those the thoughts which go through your head when I talk about only serving yourself? Time to switch this up! By serving yourself, it gives you the ability to serve others better. It gives you the time you want to serve your family. It gives you the mental capacity and the time for you to serve your clients. Serve yourself first and you will serve everyone else better!

For so long, I didn't understand this. I thought I understood it, but I was so far off. I was doing what I wanted in order to serve everyone else. This was when I was working non-stop, running myself to the ground. I thought as long as I was working to grow my business and helping my clients and athletes, I was indirectly taking care of myself.

Now that I can look back at how I was functioning, I was not serving anyone, not my clients nor myself. I was attempting to help them, but not truly serve them. And I definitely was not serving myself in any way, shape or form. I was a mess. My business was a mess!

"Do only those things that serve you" is how you serve others and yourself at the same time. It is the way in which you take care of others, take care of yourself, and give yourself time and freedom. You give yourself a better mental state!

Let's go back for a second to our schedule and our time block that we created. Those are the tasks you intended to get done on that given day. Got all those tasks done? Great!

You can stop working for the day. If you accomplished everything on your list, there is no reason you need to continue working. That is the great part about being your own boss. You aren't punching a clock; you aren't required to work a certain number of hours each week. If your work is done for the day, then stop working and go do something fun. Take some time for yourself. Remind yourself that you put those tasks on that day for a given reason and for that same reason you did not add anything else to that day. Respect that reason and be done.

Learn to shut down and relax. Personally, I have the shut down part figured out with my rules. I am still working on the relaxing part. I will be the first to admit I don't relax well. I never have but I don't necessarily think it's a bad thing.

Here is what I do, though. I shut down based on my rules I have set. Once I do that and my meal prep for the next day, that is my time to journal and read. That is my relaxation time. Everyone's relaxation time or what I also call *me time* is different. You do what allows you to relax your mind and your body.

When I first started my business, I said yes to everything. Okay, well maybe not everything, but it definitely seemed like everything. I was running a business like a chicken with my head cut off. No direction, no true vision. I knew what I didn't want — I didn't want to work with insurance companies anymore. I knew what I did want — I wanted to work with athletes. That was my focus. No specifics. No true direction on anything.

I started by saying yes to every online course I could to help me figure out how to run a cash pay physical therapy business, how to market a business in the PT world which did not require going to physician offices, and how to deal with people who had Medicare but still wanted to see me. So many things to learn, and I thought I had to know it all. While partially true, I realized I didn't need to learn it all at once.

As marketing opportunities would come up in different local publications, I said yes to those. They weren't specifically in my niche market, but I figured getting exposure wouldn't be a bad thing. Calculating it out, all I needed was two clients from each one I did for a year in order to get my return on investment. I didn't get anyone from either of those. It was a loss on all fronts. Definitely no ROI! I was learning my lesson on saying yes to everything.

Shortly after that, I was told by my husband at the time I needed to stop spending so much money, business or not, I needed to stop spending money. He saw it as an expense, so eventually I did. It got to my head. I still spent money, but I was much more cautious about it. It wasn't a bad thing to be more cautious, but it had me thinking negatively about money and using it for the purpose of growing my business.

I eventually met the man who would later go on to become my business coach. At first I was resistant about purchasing his online course. It would cost money. It would be an expense. I had invested in other courses in the past which didn't pan out and I didn't trust myself to make a good decision on this. Fortunately for me, Greg made my decision for me. He flat out told me I needed to be in. He told me he had been wanting me in the course since I met him four months prior. I signed up right away. I knew I had to do it for my business if I wanted to be successful. It was still viewed as an expense, but I knew it was an important one.

I started understanding the difference between expenses and investments. I started to learn those things which would help to grow my business were investments, but there still had to be caution. Some courses and classes are worthwhile to take based on what I need to learn; some just look fun, but not necessary for the business or myself. Marketing to my target audience is definitely worthwhile; marketing just to get my name out is not.

Going to a different area, I also said yes to opportunities that didn't reach my target market. At the time, I thought exposure was exposure, so I had to take advantage of every opportunity possible. I agreed to collaborate on projects that were not necessarily the market I wanted to focus on. Looking back, it wasn't a bad thing for me to do, it was just a waste of my valuable time. It added hours to my days and weeks that weren't necessary to be added.

So why is all this important? Because in the process, I learned the importance of saying no to things. I learned not everything can be a yes. Just because the course sounds amazing and fun, or the opportunity and project would be incredible to do, does not mean they are worth your money, and more importantly, your time, to participate in.

It is important for you to start valuing yourself. Valuing your time. Valuing what you are worth. It is important to learn to say no to things that don't serve you, your family, or your business. The only way you can begin to work fewer hours is by getting rid of those things that will not serve you in any way. It is time to stop doing things just because they look fun and interesting.

When looking at opportunities for the business, you really need to ask yourself what purpose does it serve? If the opportunity will serve your target market in some way or directly serve your business in some way, it is one you can say yes to. If you question if it will serve your market or serve your business, it is likely not something you should waste time, money, or energy on.

Here is where things can get tricky. Do you think it will serve you in two to three years? This can be a maybe, maybe not. If it is a class or conference that takes place once or twice a year, it's probably not necessary to go now. If it is something that will never come around again, or not likely to come around again, it may be something you want to invest in now.

Does all this mean I don't do anything fun? Of course not! Like I said, you still need to do the things that serve YOU!

And that means doing the things you enjoy doing, like your hobbies, recreational activities, and sports. The happier you are, the better mental state you will be in, the more focused and productive you can be.

Fortunately for me, everything flows well together. I work with CrossFit athletes and runners because I am one. So for me, I go to my gym to work out or go to group runs in the community and I am marketing myself as well as having fun and getting my training in. I participate in races and competitions for that very same reason, to get out there with my target market. To show them I am one of them.

When making decisions on anything, ask yourself:
1. Does this serve me?
2. Does this serve my family?
3. Does this serve my business?

If you can answer yes to at least one of those, commit to it. If you can't, the answer is no.

Finally, when talking about serving yourself, nothing does more for this than spending time with those people you love and those who love you. Relationships are a huge part of who we are. It took me a long time to understand this ... nearly 37 years. I spent most of my life ignoring my family and friends. I would contact them or interact with them when I had a question or needed to tell them something, but otherwise I didn't *waste my time* reaching out to them to talk. That is exactly how I viewed it — wasting my time. I didn't take time to build and grow those relationships. I can't say where this viewpoint started or how I became that way, I just did.

That doesn't mean I didn't care about people. If someone needed assistance in any way, if a friend wanted to talk, if someone was injured or ill, I was there. I was always willing to help when help was wanted or needed. I cared about others and what their needs were. I didn't care about myself. I didn't love myself and therefore I didn't serve myself.

I have learned the importance of relationships, how they serve me, and how they serve my business. Relationships are a huge part of business. If you don't know how to build relationships with your potential (or current) customers or clients, it will be difficult to get them or keep them as paying customers or clients. Learning relationships starts with learning to love yourself and learning how to love and communicate with your family and friends.

Make time for your family and friends in whatever way that looks like for you. Maybe it is reading with your kids or watching a movie with your spouse. Maybe it is spending time at the gym or on the golf course because that is where your friends are. It could be a hiking or camping trip. Whatever it looks like for you, do it! The more time you spend building those relationships with your family and friends in a way that serves you, the better you will be able to build relationships with others and truly serve them in the way they need to be served. This service of others will translate into long term business relationships for you. It all starts with the relationship!

Chapter 11: Personal Development

Personal development has been a term thrown around a lot recently. It is something that is important to do in order to grow, as a human and as a business person. I personally didn't realize the impact it would have until I started consciously doing it. Once I started working on my own development and started noticing the changes in myself and my business, it energized me to do more. It is something I look forward to every day now. In fact, my day doesn't feel right if I don't take time for personal development.

Personal development looks different for everyone. First and foremost, it has to be something that fits into your schedule. It also needs to be something that goes along with how you learn and along with the things you enjoy. If you attempt something that makes your life more stressful or you use methods that are forced, then it is not going to be effective or long-lasting. The key is finding methods you can stick with.

Personal development exists in many forms: books, audiobooks, podcasts, journaling (or as I like to refer to it now, transferring your thoughts to your "external hard drive"), breathing, and meditation are just a few methods. Personal development can also be attending courses or retreats, talking with friends, or talking with a coach. There are many different options to choose from. Personally, I do a number of them.

My day starts with my morning routine:
3:00 AM: Wake up, brush my teeth, and get dressed for the gym.
3:18 AM: Gratitude journal, writing three things I am thankful for.
3:20 AM: Thirty minutes reading a personal development book and documenting my takeaways in the process.
3:50 AM: Thirty minutes responding to messages from the night before, catching up on Facebook notifications and, if I have time, interacting with the groups I utilize for business purposes.

4:20 AM: Pre-workout food and prep gym bag.
4:35 AM: Leave for the gym.

Most successful people have a morning routine to start out their day. This routine will look different for everyone, but it typically involves personal development time of some sort. I have friends and colleagues who meditate in the morning and then spend time stretching. Another that listens to audiobooks or podcasts while going for a morning walk, a "learn and burn" as he calls it[2].

Length of time is not necessarily important, in fact the length of time may increase over time as well. Mine did not start out as early or as long as it is currently. It happened over time as I chose to add more to the routine. Initially, it was 15 minutes of writing in my gratitude journal and reading a personal development book. As I decided I wanted to learn more and grow more, I chose to increase the time I spent reading. Along with that, I know I am more alert and think better in the morning, so as I started creating schedules and limiting social media time during the day, it worked for me to add that into my morning routine as well.

Will my routine continue to change and adapt as life changes happen? Very possible. But as it stands now, I absolutely love this routine as it has been an amazing way for me to start my day and I have made amazing progress with it.

My challenge to you with this is to create a morning routine for yourself if you don't already have one. Even if it is simply taking two minutes to write down three things you are thankful for in a gratitude journal. A little gratitude goes a long way when it comes to mindset and creating the life for you that you envision. Or maybe it is just five minutes of sitting and breathing to start your day. Taking time to breathe is a great way to stimulate your parasympathetic nervous system, which is the one that relaxes and calms you. What better way to start your day than in a calm and relaxed state!

When it comes to personal development, it is best to focus on aspects of your life or business you feel are weaknesses. If you only learn about ways to improve your strengths, you are not going to make progress in your life. We are only as strong as our weaknesses allow us to be; the only way to improve, grow, and develop is by addressing those weaknesses. You may have a lot of weaknesses to address and that is perfectly fine. I know I had many when I started with my personal development journey. I still have a lot of weaknesses, but the fun part about this journey is seeing the progress you make as you work on them.

Business or life weaknesses, where do you start? You can do either … or both! Personally, I say start with yourself! There is so much interplay between your personal life and your business life, so many aspects of life in general which relate to each other. When I started working on myself, my personal self, I had no intention of improving my business in the process. In my mind, I had issues in my personal life to deal with and that is what I was focusing on with my coach and with the reading I was doing. I didn't have a clue as to how much improving things in myself would also improve the business. It was truly shocking to me. Overcoming fears, overcoming beliefs, gaining confidence, learning how to build relationships — everything was done for personal reasons, everything helped to grow my business.

Learning. Growing. Improving yourself. How do you go about this? As I stated earlier, personal development exists in a number of ways. There are a lot of methods to work on yourself. Keep it simple, don't overthink this. Some people learn better by reading, some by listening, some by doing or writing. How do you learn? How do you process information?

I do a combination of things. I know I learn better by doing and reading. So for me, most of my personal development is done by reading and writing. I write down my takeaways, the important concepts, when I am reading in the morning. This not only helps me to remember what I read, but it also gives me something to refer back to later if I want some reminders.

Yes, I have access to the book still, but sometimes it can be helpful to have the notes to refer to. Think of it as your own personal Cliff Notes version of the book.

I will listen to audiobooks occasionally if someone sends one to me that is a "must listen to," but I know I don't absorb the information as well. I will normally listen to an audiobook five to six times in order to absorb the information from it. Not that it is a waste of time by any means, but I don't always have a lot of non-focus time in order to listen to an audiobook that many times. I have colleagues, though, who absolutely love audiobooks and will listen to several a week rather than reading. It really all depends on how you learn and what your schedule allows you to do.

With that said, I love podcasts. They are shorter than audiobooks so they hold my attention better during the shorter duration. I listen to a mix of technical (PT, fitness, and nutrition) related podcasts as well as mindset and "mastery" podcasts. The other thing with podcasts for me is that many times it is a discussion rather than one person talking so it holds my attention better.

Personal development can grow into a fun time to play and create. As you learn more about yourself and fall in love with this *me time*, you can learn about how you interact with your world and work to create more incredible ways to interact with it. You can activate your subconscious and allow yourself to create some amazing things in your life and your business. The possibilities are endless!

Chapter 12: Self-Care

As humans, we know it is important to take care of ourselves. As busy humans and business owners, we often times decide it is okay to neglect our own health. And believe me, medical providers are just as guilty of this as anyone else — maybe worse! As medical providers, we take so much time caring for our patients and loved ones, concerning ourselves for the wellbeing of others, but neglecting our own. It is not really an intentional thing, it just happens. We have full schedules during our day and when we aren't working, we want to spend that time with our family and friends.

We don't schedule appointments because we don't have time, we cancel appointments because meetings or other more important matters come up. We avoid exercising because we don't have time. We eat poorly because we are constantly on-the-go. But we are feeling fine, we can see fine, our teeth don't hurt, so no need to do anything different or see someone. Right? Wrong!

Trust me, I am the first one to tell you I have been there. Maybe not with the exercise and nutrition part because that is my realm, that has always been a part of my routine, but not going to appointments, not taking care of my mental health, not sleeping, creating increased stress levels — you name it, I have been there. I learned the hard way. For me it was the emotional and mental side of me that took the hit. I have had a number of colleagues who have had their physical health negatively impacted.

Listen to Your Body

First and foremost, it is time to start listening to your body. Your body is great at telling you what it wants and needs if you are willing to listen to it. Many times, we get busy with our days, we tune in to all the external factors in our world, we go through our routines and normalcy of life that we avoid listening to what is closest to us — our self.

This is not an attempt to sound all "new-age" or "out there" by any means. It truly is just checking in with yourself occasionally and sensing what is going on. I stated earlier in this book about taking five minutes to meditate when I get home from the office. The purpose of this is to check in with myself. It was time for me to determine if I was as awake and alert as I thought I was or if I was actually exhausted. Was my brain telling me to shut down? Or was my brain saying I could continue working a bit longer?

Like I stated, for me, the impact was emotional or mental, so my check-in was more of a mental aspect I had to learn to do. For you, it may be physical. Do you feel your heart racing at certain times of the day? Do you feel aches and pains that aren't normal based on the activities you have been doing? Is your digestion weird? Are you dizzy or lightheaded? When under stress and lack of sleep, our bodies can respond in a number of ways. Start checking in with yourself. If anything is feeling off, it is time to take a break. It is time to figure out what is going on. It is not a time to continue pushing through, to continue grinding away. If you continue pushing, things will only get worse. Trust me. I have seen worse in my colleagues. You don't want worse!

Take Time for Yourself

Healthy self-care means taking care of yourself, creating time for yourself. Creating time to take care of your physical and mental health. I love using this word, **create** (if you haven't realized that yet) because you can truly create anything for yourself that you want. You just have to want to create it. Ultimately, it starts with you. It starts with you believing. It starts with you taking action.

Action can come in many forms. When creating time for yourself, you are finding that space in the day to spend time on you. Anyone can find time for anything, if they truly desire to do so. "I don't have time" is an excuse in my book!

Exercise

When thinking about physical and mental health, start creating time for exercise. The amazing thing about exercise is you can make it as simple or complex as you want. It can be as short or long as you can fit in. The important thing is finding the time to move!

Unsurprisingly, I feel exercise is important, or else I wouldn't be a physical therapist, CrossFit coach, or Running Technique Specialist. With that said, it is not just my opinion. Regular exercise contributes to health in so many ways.

The ways most people believe exercise contributes to their health include:
- Improves cardiovascular (heart and lungs) health.
- Decreases the risk of osteoporosis.
- Decreases the risk of diabetes.
- Decreases the risk of a number of chronic diseases.
- Keeps weight under control.
- Decreases risk of injury in day-to-day activities.

But it also has a lot of other benefits you may not think about:
- Helps cope with issues you may be dealing with. Many people use exercise as their mental therapy.
- Increased social interaction, as many people join gyms or fitness groups.
- Improved immunity.
- Improved quality of sleep.

And then the most important ones you may not realize, but can help to improve your productivity as a business owner:
- Increased mental focus and alertness.
- Improved concentration.
- Improved productivity.
- Reduced stress.

So what does creating time to exercise look like? It is different for everyone. It can be as simple as taking several five minute walking breaks during your work day or taking one or two five minutes breaks to do some body weight exercises, such as pushups and squats. Regardless of the job you do, it is highly productive to take short five minute breaks from your work periodically in order to maintain your focus. This isn't just me talking — there is a reason the Pomodoro Method[3] exists.

Exercise can also look like a 30 minute walk over your lunch break or when you get home from work. Or it could be 30-60 minutes at the gym before or after work. Or maybe you take your kids to practice. Instead of sitting and talking to the other parents, go for a walk or a run. Maybe you can even encourage a couple of them to join you. It is more fun and encouraging if you have a group versus going at it alone, especially in the beginning.

It can also be a combination. Maybe you have a busy day one day and can't get to the gym. Take several five minute breaks just to move around. Then the next day you have time to get to the gym in the evening. Head there after work, do not go home! Once they get home, many people with intentions of heading to the gym never actually make it. Take your gym bag with you in the morning. You are more likely to head to the gym if you go straight there compared to if you go home first.

When it comes to exercise, it is amazing for your health in so many ways. Work to create time in your day to move in some fashion, regardless of how little or long that time is. Do something! You won't regret it. In fact, your body will love you for it!

Mental Breaks

I also advise creating time for what I like to call a "mental reset" or "brain break" during the day. Our brains can only handle so much before we start becoming less productive, less focused, and less creative. The more you push through the mental fatigue, even if you don't notice it, the less productive you will be as the day goes on.

Aside from the mental rest, taking time to meditate and breathe has many more benefits than you realize, both mentally and physically.

Our bodies have what are called the sympathetic nervous system and the parasympathetic nervous system[i]. The sympathetic nervous system is the one that amps us up. It is our "fight or flight" system that is active under stressful situations. The types of situations we live in on a regular basis as business owners. The parasympathetic is the system that relaxes us, it lowers our heart rate, it allows our body to function in a more restful state. This is the system that is more active under less stressful situations. It is one that is underutilized in many people with busy lives.

Why is this information important? Because meditation and breathing stimulate the parasympathetic nervous system. By taking time in your day to meditate or do some deep breathing, it allows your sympathetic nervous system to calm down and your parasympathetic nervous system to turn on. It allows your body to function in a calmer, more relaxed state for a period of time.

Once you go back to your work tasks the sympathetic system will be triggered again which is perfectly normal. The important thing, though, is that you take some time to get you out of that state during the day and let your body's systems relax for a bit.

Meditation and Breathing

Don't care about all the health benefits? Or maybe you think it is a little too out there. Maybe this will get you! You actually gain creativity by meditating. Much of our creativity is in our subconscious. Our subconscious is an area of our brains we don't access often, especially if you are a very Type A on-the-go person, which most business owners are. I know personally it is not an area I accessed or worked to access. I didn't understand the importance. Now I do. It was an indirect result of my intentions for meditating, but something that has been so helpful for me.

Meditation helps to access the subconscious part of the brain[5-6]. It starts from the beginning, but you don't actually get good at it until later on. It is a matter of time, perhaps several months, but you will notice you are coming up with more ideas. These ideas pop up when you aren't expecting them, as that is when the subconscious comes out. What this looks like for you will be different compared to everyone else, but things like creative ideas, project ideas, better writing or speaking skills, or ideas coming to you at random, unexpected times.

I developed all of the above, but it was a realization that came later. I began to think of amazing business ideas while driving or cooking, I became a better writer, I became more insightful and aware of my thoughts and what I was feeling. My business began exploding because of everything that my subconscious was creating. It wasn't until months later when I came to realize it was the result of my consistent meditation and the ability to access the subconscious easily and consistently.

Personally, I didn't realize the impact of taking the time to meditate and breathe would have on me when I started. I thought it was crazy, but started doing it because my coach suggested it. I initially began in order to check in and see how fatigued I was at the end of the day and to determine if I could continue working or not. Later, I started to take meditation breaks to give myself a mental break during the day if I felt I was losing focus on the task at hand. Eventually, I realized how impactful those breaks truly were from a mental focus standpoint, from a body relaxation standpoint, and from a creativity standpoint. The changes I had once I created time daily to mediate and breathe were incredible.

Breathing⹁ essentially has the same effect on the parasympathetic system that meditation does, if you do it right. Everyone breathes. That is part of survival. I am talking about conscious, focused, deep breathing. This focused breathing also slows down the sympathetic nervous system and stimulates the parasympathetic system, similar to meditation. Have you ever been in an argument with someone and found yourself taking a deep breath before speaking? This is exactly why. It was your body and mind attempting to relax itself, slow itself down before reacting to the situation. It was attempting to allow you to process the situation rather than reacting quickly.

Taking time to breathe can be as simple as taking a few long, deep breaths when you notice tension building as you are working on tasks throughout the day, or if you are in deep thought and concentration. It can also be taking five minutes to just breathe. Lay down or take a seat, close your eyes, and breathe, focusing on the inhale and the exhale.

I've heard and read a number of strategies when doing focused breathing, including focusing on the pause between the inhale and exhale or thinking of the timing of your inhale and exhale. When talking about timing, I suggest either making your inhale and exhale time equal or making your exhale slightly longer than your inhale.

I have incorporated something I learned called *box breathing*⹁ in which you make all parts of the breathing cycle the same length of time: the inhale, the pause, the exhale, the pause. This can be as little as two seconds or as long as five to six seconds, depending on what you can handle. Over time, as you do more deep breathing practice, you will notice it is easier to create a longer inhale and exhale.

Whatever method you want to use for your focused, deep breathing is up to you. The important part is incorporating it into your day in some way. And like exercise, it could be different on a daily basis. Some days just taking some deep breaths while working, while other days you might be able to take a five to 10 minute break to just breathe.

Sleep

Such an important thing that most people don't get enough of, especially business owners and entrepreneurs. First off, I am not here to tell you that you must get eight hours of sleep per night. I know some people need eight hours of sleep or more every night, but I know some people wake up on their own after six or seven hours of sleep. Every person is different in that regard. I will tell you firsthand, however, that I was definitely not getting enough sleep. I was working 80+ hours a week, working until 10:00 at night at the earliest and then waking up at 3am. I did that for close to nine months because I had to. Or so I thought.

While I was doing that, I was working a contract job and building my business. Because of that, many times it was necessary in order for me to actually get everything completed for each. Even after I left the full-time job I continued my crazy hours. I felt that if I didn't respond to people in a timely manner I would lose clients. I felt if I didn't get a Facebook post done people would stop following me. I had projects I was working on. Plus, by that time, it was something that was ingrained inside of me, something I just did because it was my normal. Normal does not mean it is healthy!

There were some instances I did have to work that late if there were things that needed to get done before morning, but those instances were rare. Most times I just kept working because there were things to do, things that I didn't think could wait. My to-do list was long.

When I transitioned out of that mindset, I realized there was no reason I had to keep working past 8:00 at night when I start as early as I do. I learned that once my tasks were done for the day that I too could be done for the day.I began getting more sleep. It was up to five hours now instead of four, but more is more, right? Maybe.

At one point I realized I need at least six hours of sleep at night. I needed to find a way to create that sleep. I love my morning routine and didn't want to change that up, so the only option was changing how I approached my evenings. Once I created rules for myself to shut down earlier, I was able to get to bed and get at least six hours of sleep a night.

Why did I want to get back to six hours of sleep a night when I was functioning fine on four? There were a number of reasons. Lack of sleep or sleep deprivation long term can cause major health issues[7-8]. It can increase your risk of high blood pressure, heart disease, obesity, and diabetes. Along with that, lack of sleep and increased stress both increase your cortisol levels. Increased cortisol levels can also lead to dysfunction of many of your body's systems, as well as contribute to high blood pressure, higher glucose, and increased weight gain.

From a performance standpoint, decreased sleep can impair your focus and concentration, decrease your memory, decrease your coordination, and increase your reaction time[7-8]. You may not realize it now, but the tasks you work on daily are taking you longer than they used to. Your creativity and productivity are reduced. You cannot function as a business owner as well as you would like when you are sleep deprived. Regardless of what career field you are in, your business will suffer if you continue getting limited sleep.

As I stated earlier, the amount of sleep required varies from person to person. Work to figure out what your ideal number is. What is pretty amazing to me is once I started sleeping six hours or more per night and then had a night with only four hours of sleep, I realized how poorly I function on four hours of sleep alone. It was adrenaline and caffeine I had been living on.

Along with quantity of sleep, you also need to think about quality of sleep. If your body is not getting into or staying in a deep sleep, you will still not feel rested in the morning. Many habits contribute to poor sleep quality and many habits can improve sleep quality. Below I provide a short list of each that have helped me, but there are many more that could be included in this list.

Things that contribute to a poor sleep quality[9]:
- Alcohol
- Caffeine
- Sugar
- Blue screens (computers, tablets, phones, TVs) late at night
- Completing tasks that keep the brain stimulated

Things that can improve sleep quality[8,10-11]:
- Regular exercise
- Getting sunlight exposure early in the day stimulates your body's hormones and rhythm
- Avoiding blue screens two hours before bed
- Maintaining a regular schedule
- Avoid caffeine late in the day, limit nicotine and alcohol in the evenings.
- CBD (pure CBD is THC free)
- Essential oils, especially lavender

Nutrition

Now we come to all the things people know about when talking about health, but tend to neglect with crazy, busy schedules. The things that get pushed to the side when you are on-the-go constantly. Ultimately, if you don't take care of your actual health, you can't be there for your families or for your business. Something will give eventually, your health will suffer in some way, it is only a matter of time. Don't let that person be you!

Our bodies can only perform as well as the foods we put into them. Provide them with quality foods with good nutrients, healthy fats, and the things that support our bodies, and your body will respond accordingly. Provide it with processed foods, fast foods, or poor choices when eating at business dinners, and your body will respond to that. You truly are what you eat. The other important thing to point out with this is when you have good nutrition, your brain power and focus is greater as well. As a business owner, it is important to be on the top of your mental game at all times.

What healthy eating looks like for each person is going to be different. We all have foods we don't like. We have different schedules and lifestyles than our peers and colleagues. There are no set-in-stone rules when it comes to proper nutrition, but there are some general guidelines I suggest:

1. Consume at least three different vegetables each day
2. Consume at least one fruit each day
3. Consume at least one healthy fat each day
4. Consume healthy proteins regularly
5. Avoid fried foods
6. Avoid processed foods
7. Avoid added sugar

Fruits and vegetables are where we get most of our vitamins and minerals. For our body systems to function properly, we require the different vitamins and minerals on a regular basis, a daily basis. Yes, we can survive for a period of time without these, but eventually your body will tell you it needs them. It will tell you in the form of medical conditions. For some people it is a couple months, for some it is years, but it will happen if you continue to lack proper nutrients.

The reason you want to mix up the fruits and vegetables you consume is because they all have different vitamin and mineral content in them. The best way I can put it is to "Eat The Rainbow." As you get the different colors of fruits and vegetables in you, you will get the proper mix of vitamins and minerals in you as well.

For years, we were told to avoid eating fat. So we did! Now, it is time to start integrating them back into your life in the form of healthy fats. Not all fats are created equal. When I talk about healthy fats, I am talking about the Omega-3s, the monounsaturated fats, and also some saturated fats that have been found to have great health benefits.

Now that we got all the technical words out of the way, what does this mean? It means consuming things like olives or olive oil, avocado, nuts and seeds, coconut or coconut oil, or fatty fish, such as salmon or halibut (both of which should be Alaskan or Pacific, not farm raised or Atlantic) on a regular basis. Healthy fats help improve our brain power, and provide additional health benefits including lowering cholesterol and triglyceride levels, thinning the blood, preventing heart conditions, and reducing the risk of cancers.

The fats you want to avoid are the vegetable oils common in many products in our modern diet: soybean, peanut, cottonseed, sunflower, sesame, and corn. Also, avoiding anything that says *partially hydrogenated* on it.

Healthy proteins. What does that mean? Protein is protein, right? Not so fast! When you start looking at meats at the store, you will find terms such as organic, grass fed, free range, farm raised, pastured, and cage free[12-16]. Organic, grass fed, free range and pastured are always going to be your best choice. The fats which are naturally part of the meat in these animals are healthy for you. The farm raised and cage free animals tend to have higher levels of the unhealthy fats that cause high cholesterol and heart issues because of the way they are raised and the foods they consume in those environments.

If you are vegan and avoiding the meat proteins all together, not a problem. Many health benefits have been found from a plant-based diet. With that said, one thing to be aware of is you are lacking some of the essential amino acids the body requires to function[16-17]. If this is the case, taking a BCAA supplement on a regular basis is advised to ensure you are getting all the necessary amino acids into your body as well.

Now that you know what foods to add into your diet, let's talk about what to avoid. I touched on it a bit earlier when talking about unhealthy fats, but let's dive in a bit deeper.

Business dinners happen. Fast food happens when on the go or travelling for your business. I totally understand that. There are ways to eat healthier when in these situations. The biggest thing is to avoid fried foods when making choices. Fried foods are typically fried in one of the unhealthy vegetable oils I mentioned earlier, so naturally, that is not a great option. For example, when choosing between fried chicken or fish versus baked or grilled options, always go with the baked or grilled. It will be your better choice. When talking about vegetables, most fried vegetables are ones that are not nutrient dense in the first place. Switching out to vegetables that are roasted, grilled, or sautéed will be better than the fried variety.

When you are looking for quick meals in the form of fast food, avoiding the places that have mostly burgers and fries is advised. Most cities now have healthy fast food restaurant options. Think about the places you can get soups, salads, or sandwiches. Or the places you can create your own meal in a sense. Those are going to be better options when you need something quick.

Processed foods have very little benefit. These are the items in the middle of the grocery stores. Those things in boxes or packages. Those things that can sit on the shelf for years and still be consumed safely. If you look at labels for many processed foods, you will find added sugars, partially hydrogenated oils, ingredients you can't pronounce, and preservatives. All of these ingredients and chemicals contribute to the health conditions many people tend to experience, including high cholesterol, high blood pressure, heart conditions, diabetes, and obesity[15-16]. Avoiding these foods all together is going to be your best option, but understanding you still want to have a happy life and a social life, I will suggest you avoid them as much as possible.

Diving into added sugars a bit more, if you start looking closely, you will find sugars are added to a lot more than you realize. As I mentioned, many processed foods have added sugar, which is to be expected. Where added sugars are found and not realized as much are in bottled and canned beverages, snack bars labeled more on the healthy variety, some pasta sauce and salsas, and nutrition and sports supplements. If you really start reading labels, you will find a lot more sugar than you realize is in the products you consume. Along with that, if you like your coffee drinks, many of those are very high when it comes to sugars.

Why are sugars so bad? Studies have found that fats were blamed for high cholesterol, high triglycerides, and high blood pressure for years, turning people against fats when it was actually sugars that were the cause. Many of the health conditions in our society are due to high sugar and processed carbohydrate content in the foods we consume. Subtract that from our intake and we can minimize our risk of the cardiovascular health conditions.

Along with food consumption, we also need to think about water consumption. Our bodies are comprised of 60-70% water[18]. The exact number varies person to person due to differences in gender as well as differences between muscle and fat. This high water composition means that every single body system we have requires water to function. If our bodies become dehydrated, especially severely dehydrated, our body systems will begin to shut down. This can look like organ or system failure which can cause you to pass out.

On a less severe scale, and thinking more business related, dehydration reduces your brain power. Dehydration can cause decreased concentration, lack of focus, confusion, and difficulty remembering things[19-21]. You know as well as I do that these things will result in poor productivity, poor decision making, and poor performance. Just a 2% loss of body weight in water can start to cause these symptoms.

A human body naturally expels water on a regular basis, through our urine, through sweating, and even through breathing. It is important this water is replaced regularly. At a minimum, your goal should be to consume at least half your body weight in ounces of water each day. If you exercise, that number needs to increase due to the fact that you are sweating more[22-23].

I'm sure you are looking at that number and thinking that is huge and there is no way you can make that happen. I promise, it is possible. Some easy tips to start working on this:

1. Drink 16-20 oz when you get out of bed in the morning.
2. Drink 8 oz before each meal.
3. We've discussed taking breaks during your day to move. During those breaks, drink 8 oz of water as well.

As you start incorporating these into your day, you will notice the water starts going down more easily over time.

If you travel on planes a lot, it is easy to get dehydrated. I will be the first to tell you that I don't drink enough water when travelling because I don't want to get up constantly to use the restroom. What I do, however, is once I get to my destination I consume 32-40 oz of water to replenish what was lost. That may sound crazy, but it goes down super easy because your body is craving it if you are used to drinking a steady amount of water during the day.

When talking about nutrition and hydration, we also need to discuss alcohol consumption. I know this can be a touchy subject for people for a number of reasons, so bear with me if this is you.

Alcohol is a part of our society: for social situations, for business dinners, to destress, to relax. It is not something I will say you must avoid, as I feel in moderation and for the right reasons consuming alcoholic beverages is fine. It is when it become excessive or for the wrong reasons people start having issues.

As a business owner, you are going to business dinners or other business or networking events. Many of these events are ones in which you have the ability — and sometimes expectation — to consume alcohol. What I suggest to the business owners I work with is to be aware of how much they are consuming. It is easy in these situations to consume more than you thought you did. When in these situations, do your best to limit it to one or two drinks. Along with that, always have water with you. The consumption of alcohol contributes to dehydration. If you don't keep up on water intake, you will be even more dehydrated the next day and will be playing extreme catch up.

Aside from the dehydration, excessive alcohol can contribute to many other health conditions that I am not going to get into.

When I talk about using alcohol for the wrong reasons, I have spoken with a number of business owners who have difficulty shutting down from their work and feel guilty when they do. Because of this, they began to turn to alcohol in order to attempt to relax at night. Using alcohol for this purpose is not healthy. Over time, this will cause more issues, becoming reliant on the alcohol in order to relax, which can be a downward spiral in a *perfect storm* scenario.

If this is something you are dealing with, it is important to find other strategies to allow you to relax. I have written about a number of them throughout this book. One great one that helps with this is creating rules. If you set rules for yourself and follow them, mentally you feel less guilty when you stop working. Meditation and setting your intentions can also be helpful in these situations. I set my intentions for my day, but maybe every evening you set your intentions for your evening and what you want to get out of it with your family, with your workout, or with your personal development.

Medical care

To close out taking care of yourself, I need to touch on getting your regular medical care and check-ups. It is so easy when we have busy schedules to put these things off. It is easy to say, "I'm fine," and continue about our days.

When you are in your 20s and 30s, the likelihood of major issues is less, but still possible. Stress can cause some crazy things to happen in the body, and as business owners and entrepreneurs, the stress levels are high as you are doing everything for your business. For example, I know a physical therapist who was in his 30s, working nonstop in his career, competing in marathons, while still giving time to his family, who collapsed and began seizing, all because of the high stress levels and his never shutting down. This likely could have been prevented by destressing himself sooner, but at the same time something may have been caught if he had gone to the doctor on an annual basis for routine labs and check-ups.

As you get into your 40s and 50s, for both men and women, there are common things that may occur and regular screenings are important. If something is going on internally and you aren't healthy, you can't run your business as effectively, especially if you end up needing major medical care because of the situation or condition at hand. The sooner things are caught by regular screenings or getting to the physician when you feel something is not right, the less risk of whatever is going on turning into something severe that will keep you away from your business for a long period of time. In most cases, the sooner something is caught, the less time is needed for treatment.

When it comes to your health, nothing is 100% preventable, but the more you take care of yourself in all areas, the less at risk you are of developing something major with your health that will take you away from your business and your family long term.

Section 4: Creating Your Mindset

Mindset. Mindfulness. Awareness. All words that come to mind when I think about how someone goes throughout their day, how someone interacts with others, and how they interact with their world. These interactions can be very positive or they can be very negative. The difference can be based on how you are *being* in those situations, or the difference can be how you perceive the situation. So many factors play into this.

I like to use the words **react** and **respond** when talking about dealing with situations and people in our daily activities. I use **react** as the instinctual things that happen in any given situation. Many times, these reactions are negative: anger because of what someone did or said, raising your voice at someone due to their action (or maybe inaction), getting frustrated with someone not doing their job or holding up their end of an agreement. The list could go on and on.

Respond, on the other hand, is what YOU do. This is you making a conscious decision on how you are acting or being in the situation. This requires awareness, patience, mental processing. This requires you to function on a higher level. This requires practice and repetition. It is something that is difficult, but it gets easier and quicker with time. It is something I continue to work on daily.

Creating the right mindset, developing mindfulness, and developing awareness takes time, takes work, and it takes discipline. This is where personal development is important. Without that time for personal development, you will not grow in this area. It is not that you can't, but more of a matter of you don't know how. Like anything in life, if you want to learn how to do something or become better at it, you first need to learn how to approach it and then you need to implement.

Along with personal development, there are also some great habits to get into on a daily basis that will help you with your mindset, mindfulness, and awareness. They are things I have learned about from the continual personal development I have done. They are things I have incorporated into my life in order to be the human I want to be.

Chapter 13: Create YOUR World

You have the power to create what you want from your day. I know it sounds crazy and out there. I thought the same thing. I thought the day happened around me and I react accordingly based on the world around me. In a sense, that is true. Circumstances, situations, and events around us are out of our control. People are going to do what they want to do, when they want to do it. We cannot control other people. What you can control, though, is how you act in those situations, how you are being. (Being: a word I have come to love when talking about our presence in situations.)

Let's start with an everyday life situation: driving. Driving can be frustrating. People around you, going slow, going fast, cutting people off, turning when you aren't expecting them to. So many situations can occur in a given moment. When you are driving and someone cuts you off, you can react in anger, which creates a horrible rest of the day as you are now in a negative, angry state, or you can respond positively. There are so many scenarios why the person could have cut you off (aside from being distracted by a cell phone). The person could have legitimately not seen you, maybe they are in a rush because of an emergency situation, maybe it is something else in the universe telling you to slow down. The possibilities are endless.

Let's bring this into the business realm. I have a great example of how I reacted and what I ended up doing to recover because of my reaction. This was before I learned how to handle my reactions and was in the early stages of me beginning to work on myself.

When I was working my contract job, I had a front office employee shred some documents I was wanting back. She had already scanned them in so the information wasn't lost, but the disposal of the documents was going to make my work more difficult. I became very frustrated with her, voiced my frustration and the increased work I now had, and let myself dwell in a very negative mental state. It was not a good, productive state for me to be. That negative state added more time to the task I was completing because I was not focused. A couple hours later, after completing my work and having time to process the situation and my response to it, I realized my negative reaction was inappropriate and unprofessional. I apologized to the employee for my response.

So coming back to the *how are you being* concept in situations and how your awareness can play a huge role. You will never be able to control what other people do, like in these two examples, they did what they did. But your awareness of how you are being and how you are responding will determine how the rest of your day will go.

So how do we create this new mindset? It starts with investing time in yourself in the form of personal development, but it continues with the creation of new habits, creating a new normal.

Setting Intentions

Start off with setting your intentions for the day. I set mine every morning on my way to the gym. Driving is a great time for me to access my subconscious and develop an amazing intention for the day. These intentions don't have to be anything earth-shattering, they can be simple and basic. When setting your intentions, think about what you want to get out of the day, how you want to experience the day, how you want your day to go, how do you want to be. So many possible experiences to create when setting your intentions; they are literally endless.

Sound difficult? Start here. Think about what you have scheduled or planned for that day. Based on those things, how do you want them to go? Have a lot of meetings? Maybe your intention is to be fully present and focused in each one. Or know you have a family situation to deal with later in the day? Maybe your intention is to respond in a loving manner. You can set your intention for the day or for one specific situation. They are your intentions.

This whole process started for me when I was going into a day with my business team that I knew was going to be a highly stressful, highly emotional day. I did not set intentions at that time. I went for a run that morning in order to clear my head and to reflect on some things from the day before that I had been dealing with. As I did that, I knew I needed to enter the meeting fully present. I decided at that moment to create my day, how I was going to be in the meeting, how I was going to serve my peers. The day was amazing! Everything went as I had envisioned it. I created the day I wanted and it happened.

That was the first time I set my intentions for the day. I haven't missed a day since. And every day I do this turns out incredible.

As you set your intentions for the day, you naturally create the mindset for the day at the same time. When you have your intentions, your mindset automatically switches to whatever your intentions are that you set. Whether you realize it or not, you become focused, positive, and ready to enter your world in an amazing headspace. Without realizing it, you will start living out your intentions you have set. Once you set them, they become part of your subconscious and you just start being in the way you have set forth.

Now that you have your intentions set and your morning routine compete, it is time to settle into your day. By now, you have learned the importance of creating a schedule and time blocking your schedule. This is where it becomes important. It is now time to dial in, to focus on what you have scheduled, and get to work.

Now is when you see amazing things happen. As you settle into your day and get to work, it's likely you have forgotten about the intentions you set. I know I do by the time I start any of my focused, deep thinking work. But your subconscious has not forgotten. It knows exactly what you created earlier, it knows how you intend to be and act. Without realizing it, as you complete your tasks, interact with others, and carry on with your normal day-to-day activities, that intention will naturally emerge. It is actually pretty amazing to reflect at the end of the day and realize everything that happened in your world that day and how you created it with the intentions you set.

Meditation

Meditation is a great thing to begin to incorporate as you work to create you day, create your life, and create your world. I will be the first to admit I used to think meditation was totally out there. I didn't realize what it can actually do for you. I actually started to meditate just for the purpose of checking in with my body and figuring out if I was exhausted and needed to shut down for the night or if I could continue working. That turned into taking time to reset and recharge during the day if I felt drained, especially if I needed a break from a social situation or stressful situation that had drained my energy. I also used it to calm me down and create clarity in situations that caused me frustration.

Since then, I have learned about what happens in the body and brain with meditation[1,5,6]. I have learned how it creates mindfulness and awareness. I have learned how it helps to access the subconscious. I have learned how my entire day can be a meditation by being in the right mindset and state of awareness.

So how can meditation help you in your day?

One thing it can help improve is your productivity and the quality of your work. As I mentioned, I started meditating in order to give my brain a break while I was doing a lot of deep, focused work. The mental break, even just five to 10 minutes, helped to keep my quality of work high, as I didn't lose focus on what I was doing since I allowed myself the brief break to not think temporarily.

Along with that, when you are stressed, frustrated, dealing with an intense situation in your work life or personal life, taking time to meditate can actually calm you down. Because of how it stimulates the parasympathetic system, it creates a relaxation in your body and a sense of calm. This can also help you to gain clarity into the situation you are dealing with. Many times, once I spend time to meditate and reflect on the situation, I end up finding a solution or answer to the situation I was dealing with.

Reset and recharge. If you are an extrovert, you may not require meditation for this purpose, as you get recharged from the interaction with others. As in introvert, you may do great interacting with other individuals, but it is draining. You need time away, time alone, in order to recharge your body. You can use meditation for this purpose as well. Having that time to separate from others, focus on your body, and focus on what you are sensing is a great way to recharge your system. I am an introvert and this works really well for me after social situations or big events, and even during the situations at times if I am able to break away for five minutes.

A great side effect to meditation is you actually become more creative at the most random times. Meditation helps you to access the subconscious part of your brain. It is a part many people don't know how to access because of the high stress world we live in. Many people are in a constant sympathetic, fight-or-flight state, and therefore only access the conscious part of our brain. By slowing down and accessing the parasympathetic system, we have access to the subconscious. The subconscious is where our creativity lies.

As you begin to meditate regularly, you will find that you will come up with great ideas at the most random times, or times which seem to be random. What happens is that while we are using the conscious part of our brain for a task, such as driving, showering, or exercising, the subconscious part is working in the background. As this subconscious works, the ideas begin to flow. I frequently have creative ideas for projects or content when I am driving, working out, and cooking. You may also find you start waking up with amazing ideas as well.

Regular meditation can also improve how you interact with others. As you meditate more, you are able to be more in tune with yourself, you are able to be and act as the person you want to be, you are able to process your reactions and responses better. As you begin to sense what your body feels like when it is getting frustrated and stressed, you are better able to pause, process, and respond in a more positive way rather than react in a negative way which you may regret. This definitely takes time to develop, but when you do it can be game changing in your daily interactions with others.

If you are new to meditation, maybe you are unsure of where to even start. I know I was. I suggest starting with guided meditations. This can get you used to meditation and start to help you get in tune with your body and mind. This was where I started and continued for eight months before I began to figure out how to meditate without constant guidance.

You can find thousands of guided meditations on YouTube. I did searches for things I wanted: clarity, calm, focus, relaxation. Pick your purpose and do a search for it. Headspace[24] is an app that you can get for guided meditations as well. It is another great option for you to utilize.

A couple other apps I have found to be useful as you develop more mindfulness and awareness are Waking Up[25] and Brain.fm[26]. Waking Up is still guided, but also gives you more time to develop your awareness and mindfulness in the moment. Brain.fm is a great one I utilize daily. It utilizes sounds called binaural beats to change the chemistry of your brain for your given purpose: relax, recharge, focus, meditate, and sleep. I use the focus one every time I am doing any work that requires concentration. It is an amazing tool to have at your disposal.

Utilize Your Breath

Breathe. Something we do on a daily basis, but not to its full potential. We have to breathe to survive. That is just a fact. We can also utilize our breath for the purposes of relaxing and calming the body and mind, to reset our system.

You may not have ever noticed, but when you are stressed, angry, or frustrated, your breathing gets more labored, faster, shorter. In these states, our sympathetic system takes over, our body goes into fight-or-flight. Because of this, our breathing is affected. You can either let the state continue or you can attempt to calm it down. One of the best ways to calm it down is by using your breath, focusing on your breath.

When you focus your breathing, the parasympathetic system is activated. As mentioned earlier, the parasympathetic slows your heart rate, slows your body down, relaxes and calms you. Focusing on your inhale and exhale will slow down, relax, and reset your body and mind. It will help you remain calm in situations instead of reacting in a way you may regret later. It will help you to slow down and process your thoughts before you speak.

When your are in a situation in which you are agitated, pause and focus on your breathing. Take a couple long breaths, in and out through your nose. You can even count with this to change your focus briefly from whatever caused the stressful situation in the first place. You will find yourself in a more relaxed state, both body and mind, in a very short period of time when you do this. From there, you are able to respond to the situation at hand in a calmer and more thought out way.

As you begin to learn your body and how it feels and responds to different situations, you will be able to get out of it faster. I have developed the awareness so that immediately upon feeling my heart start to race and my throat tighten (the first two sensations my body goes through in stressful situations), I take a couple deep breaths. Immediately, calm sets in, I am able to process the situation, and I am able to respond appropriately. It took me many months to get to that point, but it does happen the more you take time to mediate and breathe, allowing yourself to become more mindful and aware of your body.

Chapter 14: Create A Grateful Mind

Gratitude is an amazing thing. It is something that is overlooked as a way to improve our mindset, but probably the easiest thing to do to begin doing so.

You may think, "I'm grateful for things," which may be true, but until you start a gratitude practice you will never fully realize the potential that gratitude has when it comes to your life and your mindset.

I started a morning gratitude journal because someone suggested it. I was told it was what successful people did. I was told it is a good way to start the day. So I did. I thought it was dumb, but I did it anyway. Even if it didn't do anything for me, it wasn't going to hurt anything either. I started writing three things I was grateful for every morning.

Several months into it, I realized I had experienced a mental shift. I realized I was happier and less negative during the day. Not that I was a negative person to begin with, but I noticed as people complained about things or voiced their negative attitude, that I was in a totally different place. I began to find myself pondering how people can be so negative, how people can be so ungrateful. I began asking myself why people can't see the positives in situations and only the negatives. That was when I realized the impact the daily gratitude journal had started to have on my life.

Truth is, you can always find something to be grateful for in every situation. It is all a matter of how you view a situation, how you perceive a situation, and how you choose to respond to the situation. The more you practice daily gratitude, the more you will see a shift happen and begin to be grateful for things in all circumstances, no matter how bad you feel they are in the present moment.

When you come from a place of gratitude as you develop your practice, you will notice an amazing mental shift in your day and in your life. You will respond to situations in a more peaceful and mindful manner. You will interact with others completely differently by being more loving and caring. You will find yourself coming from a place of service rather than a place of need or want. As much as I didn't believe it when I started, living a life of gratitude is truly a game changer.

Section 5: Now Go Create!

It is time for you to get started! Time for you to start planning, scheduling, and organizing your day and your life. Time for you to begin focusing on those things most important to you. Time for you to create some rules in your life and follow them! Time for you to start listening to your body and start taking care of yourself.

Time for you to Own Your Day and Own Your Life!

Time To Create!

Afterward

As I sit down one year after writing this book to record the audiobook for *Own Your Day, Own Your Life*, I realize how much has changed since I wrote it. As I continue to discover more about myself, about life, and about how the world works, I adapt, shift, and grow.

Routines

Routines and schedules are important to me, as you have likely picked up. They are how I function best. I am learning, though, that sometimes routines need to change as life changes or as growth happens.

My morning routine was the first to change. As I mentioned previously, I started meditating during my day to take a break and rest my brain. I also began meditating in the evening to do a check-in with myself and notice what I was feeling. Over time, I began to realize how impactful meditation was in my life and how many amazing things it was creating. Because of that, it became a part of my morning routine. I didn't add any more time to my morning routine, but I did shift things around a bit. I still wake up at 3:00 AM during the week. I still read for 20 minutes every morning. Right after I read, I now meditate for 15-20 minutes. Because I didn't add time to the routine, I had to change something. Originally, I was taking time to catch up on Facebook. I still do a little of that, but not as much; I pushed that to a little later. Now I mostly catch up on messages from the evening before I didn't respond to, or that came through overnight.

Now, time for the BIG mindset shift when it comes to my morning routine. There have been times my alarm has gone off and I was still exhausted. In the past, I would ignore what I felt and get up anyway because my routine said that I had to. It took me a long time to realize something very important—I created my routine for a reason, I can just as easily change it as I needed or wanted to as well. I realized (or perhaps it finally clicked) that I am the creator of my life and it is up to me to do things for myself that serve me best. I am the only one that knows what I need. If I don't start controlling it, no one will.

My evening routine has changed as well. This didn't change drastically, as I didn't add anything to it. I instead shifted things slightly. My goal now is to be in bed by 8:00 PM to journal and read and have the lights out by 8:30 PM. If my schedule allows me to get to bed before that, even better!

Serving myself

As I started listening to what my body needed in the mornings, I also began to learn to start listening to my body, my wants, and my desires at all times. After conversations with my coach and breaking through some mental barriers, I started asking myself, "What do I want?" in most (if not all) circumstances. Overcoming this barrier has created a big shift in not only my mindset, but also my life.

I had been taking breaks to meditate and rest in the middle of the day if I **had the time** for it, or I felt I **needed it**. Now I am creating time for it daily. I am taking 30 minutes after I eat lunch to meditate, breathe, and sit in stillness. I realized how much more creative and productive I am with these meditation breaks and how impactful they are for both my professional life as well as my personal life. It was time to make it a priority.

In the summer of 2019, my coach challenged me to shut my phone off and disconnect from the world for a day. I accepted that challenge. I noticed how gratifying it was when I did that. It was extremely relaxing to be able to fully disconnect and be fully present with myself. I also realized I didn't miss anything, and that the world didn't end when I disconnected for a period of time. No emergencies, no important messages, nothing I needed to respond to.

After that challenge, I continued to shut my phone off for periods of time on the weekends. I also began completely shutting down from work on Saturdays, and I frequently shut down from social media as well on these days. I train and coach in the morning, but once I am finished with that and do my workout post for the day, I am done working and often times off social media for the rest of the day. It took a challenge to get me to the place where I feel comfortable completely shutting down from work and from the world, and I am so grateful for that challenge. Creating this time for myself has been highly positive for me.

Realizing how gratifying it can be to not be connected to a phone, I have come to dislike the phone at times. Yes, I know I need to have it for my business, but I am taking time to completely disconnect from it for periods of time during the day. Not only will I shut it off, but I will occasionally leave it in another room so I don't see it. I have also gotten rid of my smartwatch. I wanted to do everything I could to not feel connected to my phone. The watch had to go!

When talking about listening to my body AND doing what I want, this carries over to my training as well. I typically do double workouts three days each week. Even when I wasn't feeling totally energized and ready to train, I would still go train both times. There were two reasons for this: 1) It was my routine to do so, and 2) People expected me to go to the later workouts.

The clinician and coach in me knows how ineffective training is when the body is fatigued and exhausted. I would tell any of my athletes to not train and instead rest if they were in the same boat, yet I wasn't listening to myself. I started listening to my own advice. I started listening to my body instead of my mind. This was a huge shift for me and my life! I was mentally overcoming my mental need to follow a set routine or schedule, but more importantly for my training and competing purposes, I was becoming a better athlete because I was giving my body the rest that it wanted, and the rest it needed.

The other important aspect to my training that I mentioned: people *expected* me to go. I have lived based on expectations for a long time. I thought I was past that, but obviously I was not. I was still doing things because the coach expected me to be there. I had not actually registered, signed up, or committed to anyone or anything. It was just an expectation they had. Or perhaps it was an expectation I put on myself. Either way, it was an expectation of some sort, not an agreement. It was not something I was required to do. I stopped doing what someone expected me to do and started doing what I wanted to do when it came to my training.

Mental Fatigue

We all get mental fatigue from time to time, some days being worse than others. From a recent conversation with my coach, it was brought to my attention that when I am mentally fatigued, my thoughts and words are not very clear. Responding to the same question in the evening compared to the morning brought completely different answers.

As he said to me, "those responses sounded like they came from two different people." That was the switch I needed to help me shut down sooner in the evenings when necessary. From that conversation, I learned to notice what my body is feeling when I am mentally fatigued. This helps me to understand and know when I am good to respond to messages and when it will be best to wait until the morning to do so. I do the same thing for phone calls. I won't even answer the phone for friends and family anymore in the evenings if I know I am mentally fatigued and will not be thinking or speaking as clearly.

Takeaways

It almost seems crazy and impossible when I reflect on all the big mindset changes I have had in one year, but I know the work I put in over the past year to create these changes in myself.

The biggest takeaways for both myself and you the reader:
- Each day, you are a slightly different person and need to adapt to situations based on what your body is telling you.
- You can only level up your life if you invest in yourself and do things that will help you grow.
- Finding time to breathe, be still, and meditate will enhance all areas of your life.

January 2020

Other Resources

Website:
https://www.getyourfixpt.com

Facebook:
Obstacle Course Racing (OCR) Athlete Health and
Performance Group

Instagram:
@the.ocr.doc

Highly Functional Podcast:
http://www.highlyfunctional.org

Contact:
brianne@getyourfixpt.com

References

1. Munsey, R. (2018). *F*ck your feelings: Master your mind, overcome self-doubt, and become a more significant human.* VA Beach, VA: Strong House Press.
2. Archer, J.
3. The Pomodoro Technique® - proudly developed by Francesco Cirillo | Cirillo Consulting GmbH. (n.d.). Retrieved from https://francescocirillo.com/pages/pomodoro-technique
4. Cohen, W. (1999). *Neuroscience for rehabilitation.* Philadelphia: Lippincott Williams & Wilkins.
5. Using Meditation to Access the Subconscious. (n.d.). Retrieved from https://www.selfgrowth.com/articles/using_meditation_to_access_the_subconscious
6. Hrala, J. (n.d.). People Who Meditate Appear to Be More Aware of Their Unconscious Mind. Retrieved from https://www.sciencealert.com/meditation-might-make-you-more-aware-of-your-unconscious-brain-study-finds
7. How is the body affected by sleep deprivation? (n.d.). Retrieved from https://www.nichd.nih.gov/health/topics/sleep/conditioninfo/sleep-deprivation
8. FNP, K. D. (2018, January 25). Sleep deprivation: Causes, symptoms, and treatment. Retrieved from https://www.medicalnewstoday.com/articles/307334.php
9. Altun, I., Cinar, N., and Dede, C. (2012) The contributing factors to poor sleep experiences according to the university students: A cross-sectional study. Retrieved from https://www.ncbi.nlm.nih.gov/pmc/articles/PMC3634295/
10. Twelve Simple Tips to Improve Your Sleep. (n.d.). Retrieved from

http://healthysleep.med.harvard.edu/healthy/getting/overcoming/tips
11. How to Improve Your Sleep Quality. (n.d.). Retrieved from https://www.sleep.org/articles/improve-your-sleep/
12. Grass-Fed vs. Grain-Fed Beef - What's the Difference? (n.d.). Retrieved from https://www.healthline.com/nutrition/grass-fed-vs-grain-fed-beef
13. Shain, & Susan. (2016, July 13). You're Wasting Your Money on Cage-Free Eggs. Here's What to Buy Instead. Retrieved from https://www.thepennyhoarder.com/food/cage-free-vs-free-range-vs-pastured-eggs/
14. PatiryMegan, M. (2018, March 19). Stop Wasting Your Money on Cage-Free Eggs - Here's What to Get Instead. Retrieved from https://blog.paleohacks.com/cage-free-free-range-pasture-raised/
15. Vogel, L. (2017). *The keto diet: The complete guide to a high-fat diet: With more than 125 delectable recipes and 5 meal plans to shed weight, heal your body, and regain confidence.* Las Vegas: Victory Belt Publishing.
16. Cordain, L., & Friel, J. (2012). *The Paleo diet for athletes: A nutritional formula for peak athletic performance.* Emmaus, PA: Rodale.
17. Johnson, J. (n.d.). Animal vs. plant protein: What is the difference and which is best? Retrieved from https://www.medicalnewstoday.com/articles/322827.php
18. Perlman, H., & Usgs. (n.d.). The water in you. Retrieved from https://water.usgs.gov/edu/propertyyou.html
19. Kelly, L. (2018, July 31). Even a little dehydration can impair focus, motor function, study shows. Retrieved from https://www.washingtontimes.com/news/2018/jul/31/study-even-little-dehydration-can-impair-focus-mot/

20. Nauert, R. (2018, August 08). Dehydration Influences Mood, Cognition. Retrieved from https://psychcentral.com/news/2012/02/20/dehydration-influences-mood-cognition/35037.html
21. Popkin, B., D'Anci, K., and Rosenberg, I. Water, Hydration and Health Retrieved from https://www.ncbi.nlm.nih.gov/pmc/articles/PMC2908954/
22. Water: How much should you drink every day? (2017, September 06). Retrieved from https://www.mayoclinic.org/healthy-lifestyle/nutrition-and-healthy-eating/in-depth/water/art-20044256
23. How Much Water Should You Drink Per Day? (n.d.). Retrieved from https://www.healthline.com/nutrition/how-much-water-should-you-drink-per-day
24. Meditation and Sleep Made Simple. (n.d.). Retrieved from https://www.headspace.com/ (19)
25. Waking Up with Sam Harris - Discover your mind. (n.d.). Retrieved from https://wakingup.com/ (20)
26. Music to improve focus, meditation & sleep. (n.d.). Retrieved from https://brain.fm/ (21)